G000124413

Over the Garden Wall ..

"OVER THE GARDEN WALL."

CAST OF CHARACTERS.

REGINALD DE JONES.—Manager and billposter.
EVANGELINE DE JONES.—His wife; the most beautiful woman in
America.
UNCLE REUBEN WAYBACK.—'Nuff said.
M'LLE ARABELLA VICTORIA MAUD.—An imported living picture model.
MME. PAULINA SQUALLINA.—The great French song-bird.
LITTLE WILLIE WINKLE.—An infant prodigy.
CYNTHA SNIGGINS.—From Pine Valley, who just loves the "dear men."
BUM BUM, ⎫
PRETTY THING, ⎬ Three little maids from school.
PEEK-A-BOO, ⎭
LILY ANN LONGTREE.—England's "Jersey Lily."
CHORUS.—Three ladies and three gentlemen.
TWO PAGES.

TIME OF REPRESENTATION.—One hour.

SCENE.

THE GARDEN WALL.—About five feet out from the wall of the stage,
place two upright pieces of wood about twelve feet apart. Nail solid
top and bottom. Five feet from the floor nail a piece of scantling from
post to post, and on that tack the wall, which is made of dark red cam-
bric, painted in white stripes to represent bricks. Make the wall
twelve feet long (or longer if the stage be wide) and five feet high.
Draw the cloth down tight and tack to the floor. Trim the posts and
back wall with large branches of willow or evergreen. Running vines
can be tacked to the scantling and hang down over the wall. Back of
the wall and close to it, place three boxes, each eighteen inches high,
and lay a heavy plank across them to form the platform for the chorus
and performers to stand on. Drape each side of the posts with cur-
tains to the side walls. The burlesque can be given without a front
curtain, but it is better where one is used.

PROPERTIES.

Chair in front of wall, L, for EVANGELINE. Large bow and arrow.
Lighted lantern. Hand mirror. Powder puff. Fan. Shawl. Small
curtain or sheet for the pictures. Old boots and shoes for opening
chorus.

P S635
z 9 F3z54

COSTUMES.

REGINALD DE JONES.—Black coat ; white collar. Black tie. Long hair and high hat.

EVANGELINE DE JONES.—Large figured calico dress looped up over white or colored skirt ; big hoops. Big bonnet trimmed with flowers and feathers. Very grotesque.

UNCLE REUBEN WAYBACK.—Dark pants. Linen coat. Dark shirt. Paper collar. Gray wig and chin whiskers. Straw hat. Spectacles.

M'LLE ARABELLA VICTORIA MAUD.—A tall, slender girl. Hair done high on head, with two cork-screw curls in front of ears. White waist with tight sleeves.

PAULINA SQUALLINA.—Any odd bright waist, lace trimmed, and any quantity of jewelry. Feathers in hair.

WILLIE WINKLE.—Very tall man. Smooth face. Short pants. Calico waist. Yellow hair. Little boy's cap. Must appear to have outgrown his clothes.

CYNTHA SNIGGINS.—Any old-fashioned dress. Bonnet and cork-screw curls. Fan. Very giddy.

BUM BUM, PRETTY THING, PEEK-A-BOO.—Three men or boys dressed in calico dresses ; hoops ; sun-bonnets or shakers ; palm-leaf fans.

LILY ANN LONGTREE.—Young lady. Light dress, trimmed with all kinds of colored ribbons. Hair in curls or braids. Over-dressed, and in very bad taste.

CHORUS.—*Ladies.*—Blue and white gingham pinafores with long sleeves. Large straw hats tied under chin with bright-colored ribbons. *Gentlemen.*—Blue checked blouses. Big straw hats.

PAGES.—Bright colored waists. High fools' caps made of white paper.

NOTE.—Any number of recitations and songs can be used in the performance of "Over the Garden Wall," and the order of the programme can be changed to suit the occasion. Several parts can be played by the same person, and some can "double" with the chorus if necessary.

"OVER THE GARDEN WALL."

SCENE.—The garden wall. Branches of willow or ever-green at sides and back of wall. At rise of curtain the prelude to the song "Over the Garden Wall" is played by the pianist. REGINALD DE JONES *appears back of wall in centre.*

REGINALD. Ladies, gentlemen and all fellow-citizens assembled before me to-night,—I take great pleasure in introducing to your notice the greatest travelling aggregation of the day. It has taken years of labor to form this gigantic company of "Stars," and there has never been seen such an array of beauty, grace and talent combined as you will find in this company. It is very seldom that we ever play in a town of *this* size, but last week when we were playing in Blueberry Corners, (*or name of some village near by*) we located this town on the map and decided to make it our next stand, provided we could get a sufficient guarantee from the management of this house. We are the only company on the road travelling on what is now the popular mode of locomotion—namely, the "byke"; and could you see us when we start out you would discover that we all wear bloomers. Now, I am the manager, proprietor, and bill-poster of this organization, and my wife, Evangeline, is the treasurer. I wanted that office myself; but as she furnished the money to start us out, she insists on handling all the cash. She also has full charge of the programme ; and if you will give us your kind attention we will now proceed. (*Calls,* L.) Evangeline, my love !

EVANGELINE (*outside,* L.). Yes, Reginald, my dear.

REGINALD. You may appear in front of the wall.

[EVANGELINE *ENTERS,* L.

This fair creature, ladies and gentlemen, is considered by the press and the public to be the most beautiful woman before the American footlights to-day. (*To her.*) Evangeline, my love, salute the ladies and gentlemen, especially the gentlemen.

[*She bows two or three times.*

Now, you may proceed with the programme while I go out and look after the proceeds of the box office.

[*EXIT down behind the wall.*

5

EVAN. (C.). Ladies and gentlemen,—You are no doubt assembled before me to-night, expecting to hear an ordinary Metropolitan Concert Company ; but you are not, *decidedly* not. We do not for a moment class ourselves with *such* talent as you will usually find in that class of entertainments. Our artists are selected with a view to pleasing the public, and we endeavor to secure only people of fine figure and handsome face, as you will soon see. I will not dwell longer on the merits of the company, but will, with your kind attention, proceed with our programme, which will be opened with a song by the whole chorus. If there are any bald-headed men or dudes in the audience, please do not wink at the chorus-girls, for they are very susceptible. (*Calls.*) Are you ready ?

CHORUS. Ready !

EVAN. Appear.

> [CHORUS *of six appear back of wall during the prelude on the piano, and sing the opening song. Keep the hands and arms at the sides, and on the hands of each have an old pair of boots or shoes. One or two can put long white or colored hose on arms and low shoes on hands. At the close of the third chorus, all step down backward off the platform behind the wall, and all throw the arms above the head, being careful to keep the head down behind the wall. The effect is very comical from the front.*

OPENING CHORUS : *" Over the Garden Wall."*

I.

We're the jolliest folks you ever did see,
　　Over the garden wall ;
We all are handsome as handsome can be,
　　Over the garden wall.
Perhaps when you see how happy are we,
　　You will be glad that we gave you a call ;
We'll try hard to please
While the soft evening breeze
　　Blows over the garden wall.

CHORUS.　Over the garden wall,
　　The jolliest folks of all,
　　There never was yet
　　So jolly a set,
　　And you can bet
　　You'll never forget
　　The night that we together met,
　　Over the garden wall.

II.

We'll all appear on the other side,
  Over the garden wall ;
Perhaps some fellow can choose a bride
  Over the garden wall,
Or, if any young girl should chance to see
A man whose wife she's willing to be,
Just wink your eye, we'll meet you at three,
  Over the garden wall.

    Cho. Over the garden wall, etc.

III.

Now, other people will soon appear
  Over the garden wall ;
We want you all to give them a cheer
  Over the garden wall,
We know you'll agree that we sure will be
  The liveliest, best folks of all,
So now we'll proceed our programme to read
  Over the garden wall.

    Cho. Over the garden wall, etc.

    [Chorus *disappears behind wall.*

EVAN. Uncle Reuben Wayback will now electrify the audience with one of his popular, pathetic tunes. (*Calls.*) Uncle Reuben !

UNCLE R. Ready !

EVAN. Appear.   [*He appears back of wall,* C.

UNCLE R. Hello, everybody ! Wal, gosh all hemlock ! I wa'n't expectin' tew see so many nice lookin' gals here when I come up. How air you all, anyway ? I never see so many purty gals in all my life afore. I tell yew, yew all make me feel young ag'in. I remember when I was a young feller, there wa'n t a gal within fourteen mile o' Blueberry Corners, whar I was raised, that I didn't know ; and talkin' about your sparkin' ! Why, (*local name of some popular fellow, or* "none of the young fellers here") ain't in it with me. I know I'm gittin' old; but when I see a purty gal I begin to feel just as young as I used ter be. (*Sings.*)

    SONG : "*As Young as I Used to Be.*"

I.

    Kind friends, come listen to my song,
    I'm old and I won't detain you long ;
    I'm eighty-four, and quite a dude,
    And young folks call me Uncle Rube.

My hair, once black, has all turned gray,
But what's the odds while I feel gay ?
How I could sing a song of glee
If I was as young as I used to be.

CHORUS.   Fy de I, de hap te do,
How I love to sing for you !
How I could sing a song of glee
If I was as young as I used to be !

II.

When I was young I knew life's joys,
But now I'm old, yet I'm one of the boys ;
I could téll a story, or sing a song,
With any young fellow that came along.
I could throw a ball or crack a joke,
And never forgot my pipe to smoke.
I'm a gay old "sport" you'll all agree ;
I feel just as young as I used to be.

CHO.   Fy de I, de hap te do, etc.

III.

When I was young and in my prime,
I courted the girls 'most all of my time ;
I'd take them out each day for a ride,
And always kept them by my side.
I'd hug and kiss them just for fun,
And I haven't forgot how it is done,
So if any girl here is in love with me
She'll find me as young as I used to be.

CHO.   Fy de I, de hap te do, etc.

[After song, he disappears behind the wall.

EVAN.   M'lle. Arabella Victoria Maud, one of the handsomest and greatest models of the present century, has been
secured at great expense—we have to pay her two dollars a
week, and washing thrown in—to pose in a series of living
pictures. In the last town we did a poor business, and the
landlord of the hotel where we stopped was mean enough to
keep our 99-cent frame and all Arabella's clothes,—or, that
is, all she wore on that "suspicious" occasion. So here she
will be forced to pose in her latest "Del Sarte" gown, and
without the frame. (*Calls.*) Arabella Victoria Maud !

ARABELLA.   Ready.   [*Soft music on piano.*

EVAN.   Appear.   [ARABELLA *appears* C. *back of wall.*
This superb creature, ladies and gentlemen, is considered the

most beautiful woman in America—present company always excepted (*meaning herself*). We picked her up in Hoboken. Salute the ladies and gentlemen, my dear, (*aside*) especially the gentlemen. . . [ARABELLA *bows right and left.* (*Aloud.*) The pages in attendance will now appear.

[PAGES *appear on either side of* ARABELLA, *with a curtain about the size of a sheet. Each takes hold of the upper corners and raises it up in front of* ARABELLA *until she is ready for the picture ; and then they lower it behind the wall. After the picture, they raise it until she changes. Repeat same as before.*

Now, the first living picture we will present is one you are all familiar with. It is "Liberty Frightening the World."

[*Picture. Red, white and blue thrown around shoulders. She stands facing the audience, and in right hand holds, high above head, an old lighted lantern.*

The next picture will be a copy of an original painting entitled "The Coquette." Mark how very coquettish she is.

[*Picture. Fan open and held at point of chin ; head on one side ; smiles. Front view.*

We will now be favored with a picture copied from a magnificent painting by Michael Angelo, entitled "Little Cupid." We are sorry, but we left Arabella's wings behind us, and you must imagine you see wings.

[*Picture. Stand, side view, in white gown. Very large bow and arrow, pointed right.*

The next will be "An Artist at Work." This is rather an original picture with Arabella Victoria Maud, for it is copied from a snap shot of herself that a kodak fiend caught of her one day last summer.

[*Picture. Faces left. Hand mirror in left hand and powder puff in right.*

We will now be favored with a copy of "Venus, in Winter."

[*Picture. Front view. Over head and shoulders, and gathered tight around just to show the face, is a large shawl. Comical expression on face.*
NOTE : *Other pictures may be added to suit the performance. After the pictures all except* EVANGELINE *disappear behind wall.*

EVAN. Madame Paulina Squallina, the nation's favorite soprano, who has lately made the great "hit" of her life in a song specially written for her, will now sing for you. Some think she will in time be able to reach higher than Patti or even Yaw. (*Calls.*) Madame Paulina Squallina, are you ready?

MADAME S. Ready!

EVAN. Appear.

[MADAME S. *appears* C., *behind wall, and sings two verses of* " Ben Bolt." NOTE : *This can be made very funny by announcing her in the rôle of.* "Trilby" *and having* EVANGELINE *act as* " Svengalli," *and at the last line or two letting the voice break. Any other old song can be used. At conclusion* MADAME S. *disappears behind wall.*

EVAN. Now, Cyntha Sniggins, who was born in Wiggletown, this state, a number of years ago (I don't know just when it was, for ancient history doesn't relate), will now appear for the first time in your town and give you a graphic description of her experience in a tunnel where there was a horrid man in the case. Cyntha was a chorus girl with the Wiggletown Opera Company last season, and if the young man in the seventh row will try, I am quite sure he can make an impression upon her. (*Calls.*) Cyntha, are you ready ?

CYNTHA. Ready !

EVAN. Appear.

CYNTHA (*appears back of wall, centre*). Well ! I think things have come to a pretty pass when a pretty and timid young girl can't go out without having all the men and boys on the street make remarks about her. Why, just as I came around the corner, a naughty man said, " Oh, look at that face,"—just as if my face wasn't as handsome as any girl's in (*mention the town you are in*). About a block farther up the street a boy yelled out, " Man wanted ! man wanted !." Now, I wonder how they knew I wanted a man ? And yet I do, and I've been looking for one for the last ten years, ever since I was sixteen years old, and I haven't found one yet. I am sure I can't understand why it is. I am so susceptible to the attentions of a young man, and yet they never seem to propose to me. But I think that I have found my fate at last. It was one time when I was going to Chicago on a crowded excursion train. Now, just imagine,— an unsophisticated girl like me going to Chicago all by myself ! I'll own 'twas an awful daring thing to do ; but I did it, just the same. The cars were full when I got in, and I walked down the aisle until I found a seat with only a man in it, and I asked him very timidly if I could please sit there, and he very politely got up, and I sat down; and he went into the smoking car, and I didn't see him after that. I sat there all by myself, and was just hoping some nice young man would come along, when the door opened and in came one of the handsomest fellows you ever saw. Oh, he was just too sweet for anything ! He came down the aisle and looked first at the seat and then at me, and finally said, " Engaged ?" Well, for a minute I didn't know whether he meant me or the seat ; so I just blushed and said, " No, sir."

Then he sat down beside me, and he did seem so nice I thought I'd like to get acquainted with him ; and I wondered how I could, for he seemed so awful bashful. Finally a very bright idea came to me. I had heard it said that all an attractive young girl had to do when she wanted to make the acquaintance of a young man on a train was just to try to raise the window and then make believe she couldn't do it, and he would do it for her. Do you know, I tried it ! It worked like a charm. That young man rose right up and put one arm back of me, and one in front, and raised it for me, and it was the first time a young man ever had his arms around me, and the queerest sensation came over me. Oh, it was just too lovely for anything ! Of course I blushed and thanked him, and we rode along until the wind blew pretty strong from that side of the train ; and I asked him if he would please put it down, and he repeated the same business with his arms, and the same sensation came back. By that time we'd become quite well acquainted, and he was just as sociable—until all of a sudden we rushed into a tunnel. You know it is just as black as night in a tunnel, and there that young man sat close beside me. Of course I couldn't see him, and I don't suppose I could have helped myself anyway, even if I'd wanted to. We'd only been in the tunnel for a minute when that young man—he—he—oh, I don't want to tell !

EVAN. Oh, do !

CYNTHA (*giggles*). Oh, no, I don't want to !

EVAN. Oh, please do !

CYNTHA. Promise you won't tell ?

EVAN. I promise.

CYNTHA (*ad lib.*). Well, then he —— Oh, I dasn't tell.

EVAN. Oh, do tell !

CYNTHA. Well, then, he —— (*Motions to* EVANGELINE ; *she leans up ;* CYNTHA *whispers behind her fan.*)

EVAN. You don't say so !

CYNTHA. Yes, he did, four times right there. (*Puts tip of finger on her lips. Sings.*)

SONG : "*An Old Maid.*"*

I.

Naughty men, just look before you,
Here's a maiden to adore you ;
Listen to me, I implore you,
While I tell my tale of woe.

---

*Words by permission of the author, W. B. Leonard. Piano copy of the music can be obtained from the publisher of this book, or from THE W. B. LEONARD Co, Cortland, N. Y. Price, 40 cents.

I have just turned " twenty-seven,"
   And my heart is full of love ;
I could make your home a Heaven,
   Come and claim your little dove.

CHORUS. An old maid, an old maid,
     That's what the people say ;
    Although I'm very fond of men,
     They never come my way ;
    They say that I'm not in it
     And look better when alone,
    So, sad and single I must stay
     Till angels take me home.

II.

Very well do I remember ;—
It was one night in September,
I was sleeping in my chamber ;
   With a start I quickly woke.
Cautiously I looked around me,
   Up I got my foe to rout ;
There a man stood just before me;
   But I didn't turn him out.

    CHO. An old maid, etc.

III.

Now a word before I leave you ;
I will try and not deceive you ;
And I hope I do not grieve you
   When I offer you my hand.
Won't you come and take your "tootsie"?
   Hush, my little heart, be still !
I will be your little "wootsie,"
   I'll be yours for good or ill.

    CHO. An old maid, etc.

                 [*She disappears behind the wall.*

EVAN. You may now listen to one grand outburst of melody by the whole chorus. This piece was rehearsed under the direction of Signor Cantsingio, the great Italian musical director and composer. (*Calls.*) Are you all ready ?

CHORUS. Ready !

EVAN. Appear.

CHORUS (*appear behind wall and sing the old familiar round,* "Scotland's Burning," *making the motions as stated below. The tune is familiar to everybody. Divide the* CHORUS *into three parts. The second part begins after* "Scotland's Burning" *has been sung twice by the first part. Third, the same. Sing three times*).

SONG.

Scotland's burning !
Scotland's burning !
Look out ! (*Look* R. *Shade eyes with* R. *hand.*)
Look out ! (*Look* L. *Shade eyes with* L. *hand.*)
Fire ! (*Turn* R., *right thumb and finger over mouth.*)
Fire ! (*Turn* L., *left thumb and finger over mouth.*)
Fire ! (*Turn* R., *right thumb and finger over mouth.*)
Fire ! (*Turn* L., *left thumb and finger over mouth.*)
Cast on water !
Cast on water ! (*Both hands extended front, palms down, and move them from* L. *to* R. *Disappear behind wall.*)
  [*For an encore, which is always demanded, the* CHORUS *appear and sing the following, to the tune of* "The Old Oaken Bucket." *Sing very slowly.*

SONG.

CHORUS. Old Mother Hubbard, she went to the cupboard,
  To get her poor doggie a B-O-N-E.
  But when she got there the cupboard was bare,
  And so the poor doggie had N-O-N-E.
        [Disappear behind wall.

EVAN. Little Willie Winkle, the infant prodigy, travels with us now. He is Madame Squallina's eldest of six children, and he will now appear in dramatic recitations. (*Calls.*) Little Willie Winkle ?

WILLIE. Ready !

EVAN. You may appear and recite "The Circus."

WILLIE (*appears in front of wall. Recites in a very drawly way. Hands in pockets, and is very awkward and silly*).

"THE CIRCUS."

  Ma said if I'd be awful good,
  She'd take me to the show ;
  Our hired girl, named Sally Rood,
  She said that I could be her beau
  She thinks I am awful silly,
  And says I'm always in the way ;
  And pa says I'm gettin' fooler
  And fooler every day.
  Ma says I'm just from Heaven lent,
  And some day I'll be president.
  Last week we had a circus here,
  It was the talk of all the town ;
  But not one with a bear or deer,
  Or ev'n a monkey, or a clown.

'Twas free, and so we all turned out,
    You'd thought it was a county fair;
The Deacon laughed so hard, I thought
    That he and dad just made a pair.
The women said, "Well, I do vow,
    I wonder what has happened now!"

When first we see'd the people run
    Dad said, he's sure it was a fight,
So we both went to see the fun
    And, gosh all hemlock, what a sight!
The crowd had gathered round the store
    Just like they do on circus day;
And down the road came forty more;
    While just behind was Deacon Jay.
He pushed along right through the crowd,
And then he burst out laughing loud.

Then dad, he got to laughing so
    That we all thought he acted rash;
And Charley Green, who's quite a beau,
    Just tried his best to make a mash.
He said, "I tell you, she's a 'bute,'"
    And others said, "She is a peach,"
When dad yelled out, "She is so cute,
    Just keep her out the Deacon's reach."
Then some one said from out the crowd,
"I shouldn't think 'twould be allowed."

I was too short to see the show,
    And wondered what the men did see.
So I says, "Dad, I'd like to know
    Whatever can a circus be?"
He raised me up; my, what a sight
    I then did see a-standin' there!
She looked quite "fly," her eyes were bright,
    And down her back was yaller hair.
You want to know what caused the fun?
'Twas just a gal with bloomers on.

                [Makes an awkward bow and EXIT.

EVAN. You will now be highly entertained with a scene
from the new and popular opera entitled "The Mik-a-deau."
The "Three little Maids from School" are by far the most attractive of all our ladies, and they have been known to make as
many as seven "impressions" on the gentlemen in the audience
in one evening. Bum Bum, Pretty Thing and Peek-a-boo will now
appear. (*Calls.*) Little girls, are you ready?

ALL. Ready!
EVAN. Appear!

[*ENTER from* R. *first* PEEK-A-BOO, *then* BUM BUM, *then* PRETTY THING. *All must run on tip-toe and shake the body and head in true Japanese style, keeping the fan in motion all the time.* NOTE: *Any one who has seen this scene in the opera, "*The Mikado," *can appreciate this burlesque if it is done well, for it is the hit of the evening.*

SONG: "*Three Little Maids from School.*" *

—*All run on from* R. *and stand side by side, holding fans straight out in front, up stage, and in centre.*

ALL.	Three little maids from school are we,
	Pert as a school-girl well can be,
	Filled to the brim with girlish glee,
	Three little maids from school.
BUM BUM.	Everything is a source of fun,
PRETTY THING.	No body's safe, for we care for none;
PEEK-A-BOO.	Life is a joke that is just begun,
ALL.	Three little maids from school.

[*Swing from* L. *to* R., *using fans.*

Three little maids who, all unwary,
Come from a ladies' seminary;
Freed from its genius tutelary—
Three little maids from school,
Three little maids from school.

BUM BUM.	One little maid is a bride, Bum Bum.

[*Runs down* C.

PRETTY THING.	Two little maids in attendance come.

[*Runs down* R.

PEEK-A-BOO.	Three little maids is the total sum.

Runs down L.

Three little maids from school.

BUM BUM.	From three little maids take one away.

[*Runs to* L., *in front of* PEEK-A-BOO.

PEEK-A-BOO.	Two little maids remain, and they

[*Runs* R., *in front of* PRETTY THING.

PRETTY THING.	Won't have to wait very long they say.

[*Runs* L. *of* BUM BUM, *bringing her in* C.

Three little maids from school,
Three little maids from school.

[*EXEUNT*, R., *after song.*

* Piano copy of the music can be obtained from the publisher of this book or from THE OLIVER DITSON CO., Boston, Mass. Price 60 cents.

EVAN. One of the greatest attractions we have is the great English Jersey Lily, her real name being Lily Ann Longtree. This lady, besides being a great English beauty and actress, is also a very fine elocutionist and sensational writer. She always writes her own recitations, some of which are very bloodcurdling, while others are of a romantic order. She will now proceed to give you her masterpiece, which is full of romance and love. It is entitled "The Romance of the Red-Headed Girl and The White Horse, or Love at First Sight." (*Calls.*) Are you ready, Lily Ann ?

LILY ANN. Ready !

EVAN. Appear.

[LILY ANN *appears back of wall, in centre, and recites the following.*

"THE ROMANCE OF A RED-HEADED GIRL."

I.

Once upon a day that was very dark and dreary,
A stranger wandered down the street, very tired and weary;
  He betook himself to thinking,
  Fancy unto fancy linking,
Wondering if a maiden with bright hair of auburn hue
He should meet there, and, just then, to make the saying true,
  A white horse should appear.

II.

Closely did he eye each female, as they passed them to and fro,
From her pretty, jaunty bonnet, down unto her very toe ;
  Till at last a lovely maiden
  (With big parcels she was laden),
And the bright, soft auburn tresses, underneath the hat she
  wore,
Caught his eye ; and he thought as he'd thought so oft before,
  " Will a white horse now appear ? "

III.

Wrapped was he in admiration as he gazed at her sweet face,
Wreathed by auburn tresses, curling, at her throat some dainty
  lace ;
  On her head, a stylish sailor,
  And a coat made by a tailor,
On she treaded and he followed, keeping her within his view ;
And he couldn't help but wonder if the saying would prove true,
  When a white horse *did* appear.

IV.

Then he glanced toward the maiden ; she had seen the horse
    appear.
And he saw the crimson blushes on her cheeks as he drew
    near.
        Then she looked up very slyly,
        And she said so very dryly,
" Don't you think, sir, I'm embarrassed just because I've auburn
    hair,
And the blushes on my cheeks, sir, are not there because I
    care
        If a white horse did appear."

V.

Her voice won his heart completely, and he asked her then and
    there,
If his home, his heart, his fortune, she would only come and
    share.
        Then they walked along together,
        Never minding cloudy weather.
She said " Yes," and they were married ; six red-haired chil-
    dren came to bless,
And the stranger now is kicking—that is, kicking more or
    less—
        Because a white horse did appear.

                                    [EXIT behind wall.

EVAN. Ladies and gentlemen,—I cannot express to you how
grateful I am for your kind attention and presence here to-night,
and of your appreciation of our humble efforts to please. It is
with deep regret that we must say "Good-night," for it is
almost ten o'clock ; and it is a rigid rule among us that we all
get our " beauty sleep " You have probably wondered how we
manage, travelling around as we do, to keep ourselves as beautiful as we are. *That* is the secret with us ; it is

        Early to bed and early to rise,
        That makes us all healthy, handsome and wise.

The whole company will now appear in one grand, closing
chorus. (*Calls.*) Are you all ready ?
    ALL. Ready !
    EVAN. Appear.
        [*All appear, some in front of wall, others behind it.
            All join in singing the old college song, "* Good-
            night, Ladies."

2

Song : *" Good-night, Ladies."*

Good-night, ladies, good-night, ladies,
Good-night, ladies, we're going to leave you now.
Chorus.   Merrily we row along, row along, row along,
Merrily we row along—
O'er the deep blue sea.

CURTAIN.

OVER THE GARDEN WALL.

We're the jolliest folks you ever did see,

O-ver the gar-den wall; We all are handsome as handsome can be,

O-ver the gar-den wall. Perhaps when you see how happy are we, You

will be glad that we gave you a call ; We'll try hard to please While the soft evening breeze, Blows

o-ver the garden wall.   O-ver the garden wall,   The jolliest folks of

all,   There never was yet So jolly a set, And you can bet You'll never for-

get The night that we together met   O-ver the garden wall....

CHORUS.

D. S.

AS YOUNG AS I USED TO BE.

Kind friends, come listen to my song, I'm old and I won't detain you long; I'm

eight-y-four, and quite a dude, And young folks call me Uncle Rube My

hair, once black, has turn'd all gray, But what's the odds while I feel gay? How

I could sing a song of glee If I was as young as I used to be.

CHORUS.

Fy de I, de hap de do, How I love to sing for you! How

I could sing a song of glee, If I was as young as I used to be!

NEW PLAYS.

THE MOST SUCCESSFUL FARCE-COMEDY ON THE ROAD.

SHE WOULD BE A WIDOW; or, BUTTERNUT'S BRIDE. (25 CENTS). An original farce-comedy *with a plot*, in three acts, by LEVIN C. TEES For laughing purposes only, 11 male, 6 female characters (can be played by 7 gentlemen and 4 ladies). Time of performance, 2½ hours. 3 interior scenes. The leading male characters (an old plumber and a good-for-nothing doctor) offer uncommon opportunities for 2 comedians; the remaining male parts will yield barrels of fun (undertaker, burglar, speculator, member of the Legislature, etc.) The ladies' characters (vivacious society girl, sprightly young widow, comic old woman, rollicking soubrette, irate Irishwoman and frothy French dame) are all first-rate, but none of them difficult. Played under the name of "At Gay Coney Island" the piece has achieved a phenomenal success. It is a laugh-producer all around.

☞ *In virtue of an arrangement with Messrs.* MATTHEWS & BULGER, *who are now playing "At Gay Coney Is.and," this piece cannot be produced professionally until the end of the season of* 1897-98. AMATEURS, *however, may produce it at any time, and without permission.*

A NOVELTY BY THE AUTHOR OF "THE SWEET FAMILY."

OVER THE GARDEN WALL. (15 CENTS) A musical burlesque, by W. D. FELTER. 6 male and 5 female principal characters ("artists"), with a chorus of 6 persons (3 ladies, 3 gentlemen) and 2 pages (little boys.) Requires no scenery—a paper-muslin "wall," decorated with a few evergreens, forming the entire stage setting. The programme consists of a number of specialties (including the author's well-known monologue, "Man Wanted," and the experiences of Cynthia Sniggins from Wiggletown) with various choruses and burlesque living pictures Almost any number of young people can take part in the show, which is warranted to alleviate the most obstinate case of dyspepsia in 60 to 90 minutes.

"We produced it here (Elmira, N. Y.) for the Y. M. C. A. very successfully. We turned people away the first night, and had a full house the second."

A MINSTREL SHOW FOR DUSKY DAMES.

THE BELLES OF BLACKVILLE. (15 CENTS.) By NETTIE H. PELHAM. A complete minstrel entertainment for female impersonators, that includes all the essential features of a burnt cork programme—bright and new jokes, droll conundrums, popular songs, graceful dances and novel specialties, with a comical afterpiece for a whole company entitled PATCHWORK, which will afford a clever medium for "specialty" stars. The book is not a string of suggestions, but an entire entertainment for 30 (or fewer) young ladies, that will run about two hours. The manuscript has been used with pronounced success in various parts of the country.

AN OLD FAVORITE REVIVED.

THE SHAKESPEARE WATER CURE. (15 CENTS.) A burlesque comedy in three acts, by "THE LARKS" 5 male, 4 female characters. Time in representation, about 2 hours. This thoroughly original piece will succeed beyond expectation, with fairly clever people in the cast. Each character is a "star," and each can make any number of "points." Staying at a water-cure establishment are: Hamlet, for his health, and his wife Ophelia; Macbeth and Lady Macbeth, for economical reasons, in need of the needful; Mrs. Bassanio, enjoying a legal vacation; the Montagues, having been disowned by both their houses, Mr. R. M has taken to the stage and is here with his traveling company and his wife Juliet; Shylock (from Chatham street) covets Portia's gold and bribes Lady Macbeth to incite her husband to the murder of Bassanio (temporarily on Blackwell's Island), so that the Jew can marry the fair heiress. All of which is accomplished, and a wedding dinner, under the superintendence of Othello (a darkey waiter), is given by the other patients to the happy bride and bridegroom.

This is a new edition, partly rewritten, of a favorite comedy that has been out of print for some years.

THE LATEST NEGRO FARCE.

DOCTOR SNOWBALL. (15 CENTS) A negro farce in one act, by JAMES BARNES. 3 male characters. Scene, a plain room with a table and two chairs. Crisp and snappy and admits of specialties. *The Doctor* has a great head for humbug, *Zeke* a great head for gymnastics, and *Pompey* a great head for business. Will

HAROLD ROORBACH, Publisher,
132 Nassau Street, - - - - - - NEW YORK.

make the audience laugh themselves sore. Runs 20 minutes, if played straight, without specialties.

A SEQUEL TO "THE DEACON."

THE DEACON'S TRIBULATIONS. (15 CENTS.) A comedy-drama in four acts, by HORACE C. DALE. 8 male, 4 female characters. Time of playing, 2 hours. This is a worthy successor to the ever-popular "DEACON," in which the old favorites reappear amid new surroundings, all of them a little older, some of them very much married. The "business" is just as forcible, the situations just as laughable and the act-endings just as uproarious as they are in the older play. *Pete* is up to all his old, and some new, tricks; *Daisy* is made happy forever, and *The Deacon* is finally and completely cured of his fondness for lemonade with a stick in it. The author confidently recommends this piece to all societies that wish to repeat their old successes with "THE DEACON."

NEW PIECES FOR YOUNG FOLK.

A FESTIVAL OF FLOWERS. (15 CENTS.) By CLARENCE F. SHUSTER. A musical entertainment for children—13 boys and 13 girls. The cast can be curtailed, if desired, by omitting some of the Flowers. Each character, representing a flower, has certain lines of recitative with appropriate "business." There are several pretty songs and simple dances (a minuet can be introduced), and the spectacle concludes with "The Flower Festival March" and a tableau representing an enormous bouquet. Time of representation, about half an hour. Colored tissue papers make the costumes, and there are no troublesome "properties." The piece is an ingenious rhythm of melody, movement and color, that will command the favor of young people of all ages.

THE CAPTIVE PRINCESS. (15 CENTS.) A play suitable for school entertainments and adapted to children of 12 years or under, by A. M. MITCHELL. 9 characters, viz.: 1 girl, 1 boy and 7 others (either boys or girls), personifying various Studies. The Princess is captured by tyrants, who bear her away to their castle, where they keep her at hard and difficult tasks. Just as she reaches the verge of despair Prince Promotion appears and rescues her from her thraldom. The piece requires no scenery nor any properties that cannot be made of cardboard easily. Contains several simple songs asd some very smart dialogue, and is singularly free from all goody-goody flavor. Plays about half an hour.

THE LOST NEW YEAR. (15 CENTS.) A play in verse, by E. M. CRANE, for young actors of 5 to 12 years. 8 principal characters, and choruses of Seasons, Fairies, Butterflies and Flowers. The piece was written for and first produced by about 30 children, boys and girls, of various ages. The cast can be made greater or smaller by increasing or curtailing the choruses. No trouble about costumes or properties. Time of representation, about 45 minutes. Master New Year, while speeding earthward, loses his way and is persuaded by the Fairies to tarry and join their ring. As the time approaches for Old Year to depart, with still no sign of his successor, the Seasons, the Flowers and the Butterflies are thrown into deep consternation, but when the alarm has reached its height, and New Year seems irretrievably lost, the Fairies bring him to take his place and receive his welcome just in time for Old Year to disappear. The piece is as bright as a dollar throughout.

THREE STANDARD SUCCESSES.

ALL THE COMFORTS OF HOME. (25 CENTS.) A comedy in four acts, by WILLIAM GILLETTE, as first produced at the Boston Museum, March 3, 1890. AUTHORIZED COPYRIGHT EDITION, printed from the original prompt-copy, 10 male, 7 female characters (by doubling, it is usually played by 6 gentlemen and 4 ladies). Costumes of the day. One parlor scene throughout. Time of playing, 2 hours and 35 minutes. Acting rights reserved.

A NIGHT OFF. (25 CENTS.) A comedy in four acts, from the German of Schoenthan, by AUGUSTIN DALY, as first produced at Daly's Theatre, N. Y., March 4, 1885. AUTHORIZED COPYRIGHT EDITION, printed from the original prompt-copy. 6 male, 5 female characters. Modern costumes. 2 interior (parlor) scenes. Time of playing, 2½ hours. Acting rights reserved.

SEVEN-TWENTY-EIGHT. (25 CENTS.) A comedy in four acts, from the German of Schoenthan, by AUGUSTIN DALY, as first produced at Daly's Theatre, N. Y., February 24, 1883. AUTHORIZED COPYRIGHT EDITION, printed from the original prompt-copy. 7 male, 4 female characters. 2 interior (parlor) scenes. Time of playing, 2½ hours. Acting rights reserved.

"All the Comforts of Home," "A Night Off" and "Seven-Twenty-Eight" are subject to a fee for production by amateurs. (Particulars to be found in the printed books.) *The publisher is not concerned in the collection of fees.*

HAROLD ROORBACH, Publisher,
132 Nassau Street, - - - - - - - NEW YORK.

TOWNSEND'S
"AMATEUR THEATRICALS.

A Practical Guide for Amateur Actors.

PRICE, 25 CENTS.

THIS work, without a rival in the field of dramatic literature, covers the entire subject of amateur acting, and answers the thousand and one questions that arise constantly to worry and perplex both actor and manager. It tells how to select plays and what plays to select; how to get up a dramatic club—whom to choose and whom to avoid; how to select characters, showing who should assume particular *roles;* how to rehearse a play properly—including stage business, by-play, voice, gestures, action, etc.; how to represent all the passions and emotions, from Love to Hate (this chapter is worth many times the price of the book, as the same information cannot be found in any similar work); how to costume modern plays. All is told in such a plain, simple style that the veriest tyro can understand. The details are so complete and the descriptions so clear that the most inexperienced can follow them readily. The book is full of breezy anecdotes that illustrate different points. But its crowning merit is that it is thoroughly PRACTICAL—it is the result of the author's long experience as an actor and manager. Every dramatic club in the land should possess a copy of this book, and no actor can afford to be without it. It contains so much valuable information that even old stagers will consult it with advantage.

HELMER'S
ACTOR'S MAKE=UP BOOK.

A Practical and Systematic Guide to the Art of Making-up for the Stage.

PRICE, 25 CENTS.

FACIAL make-up has much to do with an actor's success. This manual is a perfect encyclopedia of a branch of knowledge most essential to all players. It is well written, systematic, exhaustive, practical, unique. Professional and amateur actors and actresses alike pronounce it THE BEST make-up book ever published. It is simply indispensable to those who cannot command the services of a perruquier.

CONTENTS.

Chapter I. THEATRICAL WIGS.—The Style and Form of Theatrical Wigs and Beards. The Color and Shading of Theatrical Wigs and Beards. Directions for Measuring the Head. To put on a Wig properly.

Chapter II. THEATRICAL BEARDS.—How to fashion a Beard out of Crepe Hair. How to make Beards of Wool. The growth of Beard simulated.

Chapter III. THE MAKE-UP.—A successful Character Mask, and how to make it. Perspiration during performance, how removed.

Chapter IV. THE MAKE-UP BOX.—Grease Paint . Grease Paints in Sticks; Flesh Cream; Face Powder; How to use Face Powder as a Liquid Cream; The various shades of Face Powder. Water Cosmetique. Nose Putty. Court Plaster. Cocoa Butter. Crepe Hair and Prepared Wool. Grenadine. Dorin's Rouge. "Old Man's" Rouge. "Juvenile" Rouge. Spirit Gum. Email Noir. Bear's Grease. Eyebrow Pencils. Artist's Stomps. Powder Puffs. Hare's Feet. Camel's-hair Brushes.

Chapter V. THE FEATURES AND THEIR TREATMENT.—The Eyes : Blindness. The Eyelids. The Eyebrows : How to paint out an eyebrow or mustache; How to paste on eyebrows; How to regulate bushy eyebrows. The Eyelashes : To alter the appearance of the eyes. The Ears. The Nose : A Roman nose; How to use the nose putty; a pug nose; an African nose; a large nose apparently reduced in size. The Mouth and Lips : a juvenile mouth; an old mouth; a sensuous mouth; a satirical mouth; a one-sided mouth; a merry mouth; a sullen mouth. The Teeth. The Neck, Arms, Hands and Finger-nails : Finger-nails lengthened. Wrinkles : Friendliness and Sullenness indicated by wrinkles. Shading. A Starving Character. A Cut in the Face. A Thin Face made Fleshy.

Chapter VI. TYPICAL CHARACTER MASKS.—The Make-up for Youth; Dimpled Cheeks. Manhood. Middle Age. Making up as a Drunkard : One method; another method. Old Age. Negroes. Moors. Chinese. King Lear. Shylock. Macbeth. Richelieu. Statuary. Clowns.

Chapter VII. SPECIAL HINTS TO LADIES.—The Make-up. Theatrical Wigs and Hair Goods.

☞ *Copies of the above will be mailed, post-paid, to any address, on receipt of the annexed prices.*

HAROLD ROORBACH, Publisher, 132 Nassau St., N. Y.

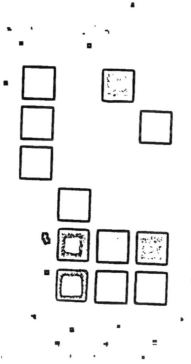

Lightning Source UK Ltd.
Milton Keynes UK
UKHW022335060223
416579UK00001B/11